GREAT ZOOS OF THE UNITED STATES™

MIAMI METROZOO

SHERRIE AVERY

The Rosen Publishing Group's
PowerKids Press™
New York

To Kevin and Cody Hudson

Published in 2003 by The Rosen Publishing Group, Inc.
29 East 21st Street, New York, NY 10010

First Edition

Editor: Natashya Wilson
Book Design: Michael J. Caroleo and Michael de Guzman

Photo Credits: Cover, title page, pp. 8 (top), 20 (bottom left and right) © Ron Magill/Miami Metrozoo; pp. 4, 7 (inset), 19 (top) © Barbara Crutchfield/Miami Metrozoo; pp. 8 (bottom), 12 (top left and bottom), 15, 16, 19 (bottom) © Sherrie Avery/Miami Metrozoo; p. 11 © Linda Crutchfield/Miami Metrozoo; p.12 (top right) © Ricardo Stanoss; p. 20 (top) © Dolora Batchelor/Miami Metrozoo; p. 7 (map) courtesy Stanford Group Company, provided by Miami Metrozoo.

Avery, Sherrie.
Miami Metrozoo / Sherrie Avery.— 1st ed.
        p. cm. — (Great zoos of the United States)
    Summary: Provides a look at the Miami Metrozoo, describing its operation, some zoo exhibits, and a variety of the animals that can be found there.
    Includes bibliographical references (p.   ).
    ISBN 0-8239-6316-0 (lib. bdg.)
    1. Miami Metrozoo—Juvenile literature. [1. Miami Metrozoo. 2. Zoos.] I. Title. II. Series.
QL76.5.U62 M533 2003
590'.7'3759381—dc21

                                2002000123

Manufactured in the United States of America

CONTENTS

Miami Metrozoo can keep many animals that cannot live in colder areas. The Zoo's apes still get extra covers in winter to stay warm.

In 1948, Chas James Ritzel and his traveling zoo were in Miami when his truck broke down. To pay for repairs, he sold an **ocelot**, two monkeys, and two bears to Dade County for $270. He included a goat for free. The county started the Crandon Park Zoo. By 1980, this zoo had 1,000 animals and needed more space. The county moved the zoo to 720 acres (291 ha) of land, where the Richmond Naval Air Station was. A hurricane destroyed the station in 1945. The zoo became Miami Metrozoo. Metrozoo is five times larger than the average zoo in the United States. It hosts 500,000 visitors every year. It is closer to the **equator** than any other U.S. zoo and is the only **subtropical** zoo in the country.

A powerful white Bengal tiger guards Metrozoo's Cambodian temple. A 400-pound (181-kg) silverback lowland gorilla boxes with his five-year-old daughter. Australian wallabies jump across the grass. A visit to Miami Metrozoo is like being on **safari** in the wild!

Nearly all the animals live in large, grassy **exhibits** with **moats** that separate the animals from people. It looks as if the animals are living in the wild. Rocks and plants hide the animals' night houses from view.

Metrozoo is set up to display animals from Africa, Asia, and Australia. Most of the Zoo's animals can be found in the wild on these continents. Soon a fourth area will be built for animals from the **tropical** American **rain forests**.

Metrozoo's map guides visitors through Miami Metrozoo. Inset: In the Zoo's Africa area, a young lowland gorilla plays with an adult.

Monorail Station 4

Guanaco/Rhea

Kudu
Thomson Gazelle
Crowned Crane

Colobus Monkey

Black Rhinoceros

Black Rhinoceros

Ostrich

African Elephant

Black Duiker
Grant's Zebra
Bongo
Grant's Gazelle
Spurred Tortoise
Giraffe
W. Crown Crane

Metrozoo Lake

Adbim's Stork
Gerenuk
White Backed Vulture
Impala
African Porcupine
Bat Eared Fox

AFRICA

Monorail Route

Andean Condor

Gorilla
Nile Lechwe

Chimpanzee
Defassa Waterbuck
Nyala

Stanley Crane

Pygmy Hippo
Monorail Station 3
Yellow-Back Duiker
Cape Teal
European White Stork
Squirrel Monkey
Gemsbok
Grevy's Zebra
Black Duiker
Arabian Onyx
Kids' Fun Center
Serval
Red Kangaroo
Baird's Tapir
Sable Antelope
Baird's Tapir
Crested Screamer
Gaur
Scimitar Horned Onyx
Koala
Sloth Bear
Dromedary Camel
Giant Land Tortoise
Concert Meadow
Tree Kangaroo
Crested Screamer
Amphitheatre
Bactrian Camel
Crocodile Monitor
Wallaby
Monorail Station 1
Himalayan Black Bear
Wart Hog
Falcon Batchelor
Lemurs
Komodo Dragon
Orangutan
Encounter
Cape Hunting Dog
Egyptian Geese
Small Reptile
AUSTRALIA
Siamang Gibbons (maorhens)
Malayan Sun Bear
Asian River Life
Otters
Addax
Dr. Wilde's World
Anoa
Onager
Blesbok
Spoonbill Ibis
White Bengal Tiger
Maribou Stork
Cuban Crocodile
Bar Headed Goose
ASIA
Dama Gazelle
Carib Flamingo
Saddle-billed Stork
Asian Elephant
Water Fowl
Malayan Tapir
Classrooms
Wings of Asia (coming soon)
Indian Rhinoceros
Lion
Special Events
Picnic Field
Gifts
Asian Elephants
Swan
Koi
Metrozoo Administration Building
Monorail Station 2
Black Necked Stork
Zoological Society Administration Building
Pony Rides (Weekends)
Meerkats
Exit Here
Enter Here
Ecology Theater

Children's Petting Zoo

East Parking

West Parking

South
East
West
North

MIAMI
METRO
ZOO

7

Komodo dragons are the world's largest lizards. A Komodo dragon can grow to be 10 feet (3 m) long.

In 1998, Metrozoo hatched 27 Komodo dragon babies from a single nest. That was a record in the western world.

Komodo dragons come from the islands of Komodo, Flores, and Rintja, which are in the country of Indonesia.

Zoos Protect Rare and Endangered Animals

Komodo dragons, tree kangaroos, and African elephants are **endangered** animals. Guanacos, camel-like animals from South America, are rare. If we do not take care of them, these animals will soon become **extinct**.

Miami Metrozoo has more than 1,500 animals representing 291 **species**. Thirty-nine of these species are endangered. Metrozoo's **breeding** programs have received many awards. Several Andean condors raised at Metrozoo have been released back into their native land in South America. The Andean condor is one of the world's largest flying birds.

Metrozoo works with zoos around the world to protect wild animals. It is Metrozoo's job to help save the wildlife for the future.

TREE KANGAROOS

Tree kangaroos move quickly and easily through the trees in the rain forests of Papua New Guinea and of Queensland, Australia. Their long, muscular tails serve as balancing bars to keep them steady on high branches while they chew on their favorite tree leaves. Thick pads on the bottoms of their feet and long, curved nails allow tree kangaroos to grasp branches easily as they climb trees. Tree kangaroos also have scent **glands** on their chests. They rub these glands against tree trunks and branches so that other tree kangaroos will know they were there. Hunters and farmers who cut down forests are endangering tree kangaroos. Miami Metrozoo is helping to save these gentle animals.

A baby tree kangaroo is called a joey. It lives in its mother's pouch for the first five to seven months of its life.

Top Left: *Meerkats eat mealworms from a melon.* Top Right: *Helpers cut up food in the kitchen.* Bottom: *A Malayan sun bear has a treat.*

It costs about $300,000 per year to feed the animals at Miami Metrozoo. They eat more than 1,000 pounds (454 kg) of grain and more than 2,000 pounds (907 kg) of meat each day. Every week they eat almost 20,000 pounds (9,072 kg) of hay and more than 2,000 pounds of fruit and vegetables. Metrozoo's kitchen staff must know the exact type and amount of food to feed each animal. They also must know the animals' growth rates, health, and tastes. Gorillas, orangutans, and chimpanzees prefer mangos, oranges, and coconuts to other types of fruit. For bears, branches and sticks are coated with honey or peanut butter. Otters dive into water to catch live fish that are put there for their meals.

Making Life Interesting for the Animals

The animals usually live longer and healthier lives in Miami Metrozoo than they would in the wild. Animal exhibits are designed for the animals' comfort. Sun bears like warm, sunny rocks, so rocks are put in their homes. Lions and tigers like to sleep in trees, so their homes have trees.

To keep animals from being bored, zookeepers hide food, such as pieces of fruit and vegetables, throughout the exhibits. The animals spend a lot of time searching for their food, just as they would in the wild.

Some animals spend time playing with their keepers. Peggy, an African elephant, plays a harmonica with her keeper. Jordan, a Bactrian camel, plays soccer with his keepers!

Animals either coming to or leaving from Metrozoo are kept away from other animals for at least 30 days to be sure they are healthy.

Jordan the Bactrian camel gets ready to nose a ball over to his keeper, Patrick.

15

Top Left: *The vet and a keeper check a baby guanaco.* Top Right: A keeper tends the gemsbok pasture. Bottom: *Dentists fix a bear's gums.*

A zoo needs zookeepers to care for the animals. Did you know that a zoo also needs carpenters, cooks, electricians, a maintenance crew, and many other helpers? These are only a few of the 220 staff members and 167 **volunteers** who work at Miami Metrozoo.

Volunteers work in the Zoo every day. Two volunteer dentists fixed a bear's gums and gave a lion two metal teeth! Cleaning the petting yard, talking to visitors, and helping in the kitchen are some things that volunteers do.

The things you learn in school are important in running a zoo. For example, the cook needs to know math to mix food for animals' meals. The **curator** must know **geography** to understand how animals live in the wild.

17

KIDS WORK AT THE ZOO, TOO!

Teens ages 14 to 17 can train to be Teen **Zoologists** for Metrozoo. They help with the summer camp programs, work in the Children's Zoo petting yard, and help the staff with special events, such as Halloween MetroBOO and Easter Egg Safari. Teen Zoologists must work at least 40 hours during the summer.

In special school programs, elementary and middle school students learn about animals, the **conservation** of endangered species, and the Zoo's role in the community. Children take classes at and field trips to the Zoo. Some work with the Zoo staff on a regular basis.

Campers learn about animals, their **habitats**, and conservation. They can make treats for the bears, such as lemonade-and-fruit popsicles.

Angolan colobus monkeys come from Africa. Newborns are solid white. They turn black by about six months of age.

At the Zoo, kids can learn how Angolan colobus monkeys and iguanas get along. The monkeys like to play with the iguanas!

Summer camper Kevin Hudson makes a snack box for the sun bears.

The dinosaur Tyrannosaurus rex may be kin to a tiny Mandarin duck! Many scientists believe that birds are related to dinosaurs. Dinosaurs died out 65 million years ago.

The Zoo's aviary, or house for birds, will reopen in 2003. It will include an exhibit about how birds, such as this Mandarin duck, are linked to dinosaurs.

Metrozoo's aviary housed 300 Asian birds. After the storm, 130 birds were never found.

Zoo flamingoes stayed safe in a restroom.

HURRICANE ANDREW DESTROYED MIAMI METROZOO

On August 24, 1992, Hurricane Andrew destroyed Miami Metrozoo. A hurricane is a storm with very strong winds, rain, and tornadoes. Rain flooded the moats. Winds of more than 200 mph (322 km/h) tore down Zoo buildings and fences. Thousands of trees were uprooted or were burned by lightning. The damage amounted to $15 million.

Twenty of the Zoo's 1,000 animals died, and 130 birds were never found. Many animals remained in their exhibits, even though the **barriers** were gone. Those that escaped either returned on their own or were caught.

The Zoo has been rebuilt to withstand hurricane-force winds. The new shelters will keep the animals safe during a hurricane.

DR. WILDE'S WORLD

Dr. Wilde's World is a new indoor exhibit that houses changing displays and two Zoo classrooms. Dr. Bea Wilde is a made-up **naturalist** who has built her office and science laboratory at Miami Metrozoo. She wants visitors to discover how animals, plants, and people live together. The first display in Dr. Wilde's World features the American rain forests. Visitors can see clothes, tools, and **artifacts** made by the rain forests' native people. They can spy on emerald tree boas, matamata turtles, and blue morpho butterflies. The exhibit is filled with the sounds of the rain forest. Dr. Wilde's World is a place for people to learn how we all can enjoy and protect the natural wonders of the world.

GLOSSARY

artifacts (AR-tih-fakts) Objects made long ago by humans.

barriers (BAYR-ee-erz) Things that block something else from passing.

breeding (BREED-ing) Bringing animals together to make babies.

conservation (kon-sur-VAY-shun) Protecting something from harm.

curator (KYUR-ay-tuhr) The person in charge of a zoo or museum.

endangered (en-DAYN-jerd) In danger of dying out within 20 years.

equator (ih-KWAY-tur) An imaginary line around Earth that separates it into two parts, northern and southern.

exhibits (ig-ZIH-bits) Displays made for people to come and see.

extinct (ik-STINKT) No longer existing.

geography (jee-AH-gruh-fee) The study of Earth's surface.

glands (GLANDZ) Parts of a body that let out sweat or other body fluids.

habitats (HA-bih-tats) The surroundings where animals or plants live.

moats (MOHTS) Deep, wide ditches, usually filled with water, around an exhibit.

naturalist (NA-chuh-ruh-list) Someone who studies and cares about nature.

ocelot (AH-seh-lot) A yellow-colored wildcat with black spots and stripes.

rain forests (RAYN FOR-ests) Wet, warm forests where many kinds of plants and animals live.

safari (suh-FAR-ee) A journey through wild countryside to see the land and animals.

species (SPEE-sheez) A single kind of plant or animal.

subtropical (suhb-TRAH-pih-kuhl) Just outside of the tropical parts of Earth

tropical (TRAH-puh-kul) Having to do with the warm parts of Earth that are near the equator.

volunteers (vah-luhn-TEERZ) People who offer to work without pay.

zoologists (zoh-AH-luh-jists) People who study and work with zoo animals.

INDEX

WEB SITES

Due to the changing nature of Internet links, PowerKids Press has developed an
online list of Web sites related to the subject of this book. This site is updated
regularly. Please use this link to access the list:
www.powerkidslinks.com/gzus/miamiz/